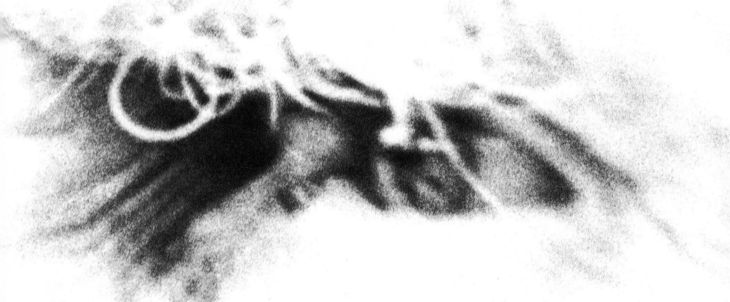

EZRA POUND IN ITALY

EZRA POUND IN ITALY
FROM THE PISAN CANTOS

Photographs by: VITTORUGO CONTINO

Edited by: GIANFRANCO IVANCICH

RIZZOLI
NEW YORK

Published in the United States of America
in 1978 by

$\mathscr{R}$IZZOLI INTERNATIONAL PUBLICATIONS, INC.
712 Fifth Avenue/New York 10019

© *1970 by Gianfranco Ivancich*

Library of Congress Catalog Card Number: LC 77-95-288
ISBN: 0-8478-0170-5

Printed in Italy

Introduction and facsimile

Ezra Pound

INTRODUCTION

These photographic compositions by Vittorugo Contino are of places and things recorded in my Pisan Cantos, places that I first saw in 1898 thanks to my great-aunt Frank. My seeing them again in 1968 was due to the initiative and energy of Contino who has shown remarkable persistence in trying to make the selection as significant as possible.

The classic account of a relation between photographer and writer is, and probably will remain, Coburn's chapter on his frontispieces for Henry James' novels. James chose photographic illustrations for these because he felt that « photographs were in as different a medium as possible ». As he wrote Coburn: « the photographic studies were to seek the way, which they have happily found, I think, not to keep or to pretend to keep, anything like dramatic step with their suggested matter ». The photographs were not to be « competitive with the text, or obvious illustrations » but to be « images always confessing themselves mere optical symbols or echoes, expressions of no particular thing in the text, but only of the type or idea of this thing or that thing ». They were to remain « pictures of our "set" stage with the actors left out ». Contino was not to be persuaded that my presence was not needed in these photographs of places; he had his own ideas and stuck to them. Asked for a title for the book I suggested « Spots and Dots », i. e. « locations and punctuations »; but though I quoted Prof. Richard Ellmann in defense of my dots, the title was vetoed as being too frivolous.

The second half of this volume contains facsimili of texts which, translated, I read in the course of interviews with Pier Paolo Pasolini and Vanni Ronsisvalle for an italian documentary. It was my first talk with Pasolini, enjoyable, if a little one sided through my fault; I would like to meet him in an atmosphere less bristling with points of interrogation. Vanni Ronsisvalle, a sicilian poet whose work merits serious attention, followed my « advice to the young » to the letter.

Gianfranco Ivancich « of the city of Aldus », where my own literary venture started, has chosen this book as the first in a venture of his own. I thank him and wish him "buona fortuna"; « things have ends and beginnings ».

Ezra Pound

« Alvin Langdon Coburn » (1882-1966), american photographer; in collaboration with the author, he made the frontispieces for the 24 volumes: The Novels and Tales of Henry James (Macmillan & Co. 1907).

« Prof. Ellmann » criticising Pound's use of « broken sentences » in « La Fraisne » says: « these are perhaps the most important *dots* in English Poetry ». (Richard Ellmann, « Ez and old Billyum »; The Kennyon Review, September 1966).

« My great-aunt Frank »: Mrs Ezra Weston, neé Frances Wessel, figures largely in « Indiscretions ». (Indiscretions, Ezra Pound, ed. W. Bird, Three Mountain Press, Paris, 1923).

My first encounter with Ezra Pound was at a Poetry Reading several years ago. He had read an Ode of Shang from the Confucian Anthology. The Ode made a deep impression [1]. His voice seemed unrelated to a body. Genius, we all felt it, was in the air. I was deeply moved. Other poets had read their own poems. The Ode, which Pound had « only translated », is from the oldest part of the Anthology, more than a thousand years B. C.[2]. His humanity showed in his reading this. In the Preface to his italian translation of Pound's version of the Anthology, Carlo Scarfoglio [3] defines it as « a contribution to the Humanistic Culture of the World understood as History of Mankind.

These things led what was then only my « reporter's » instinct into considering the possible interest of a visual interpretation of my sensations. I meditated on the matter for some years, observing, testing my instinct. Then I found in a line in Pound's first book, *A Lume Spento,* both my own hesitancy and certainty; « In vain have I striven to teach my heart to bow » [4].

I decided to show Pound the man, now at the end of his life, without thoughts of his past. To take him to places recorded in his « Pisan Cantos » [5] for my camera to catch his reactions. I confess that its mobility did not equal Pound's penetrating eye which pins down thoughts, strips a conscience bare, with the same thoroughness as do his words. Olga Rudge seconded my project and I got a pointer from her: « you see, E. P. may seem detached, no longer interested, on the contrary he follows everything; think of an automobile with the motor running, it is not moving but it is functioning ». This is how the conversation started.

I had proposed to myself a methodical piece of work; my thesis « the Portrait of a Genius » [6]. Pound took me up to the very highest roof terraces in Venice; on the way I made my first moves. Then Olga Rudge: « because... you understand... », with great kindness, turned down my thesis. I now saw that the question was whether Pound would consent. I was up against reserve humility, modesty, manners-all his real personality. The discussion widened; more meetings, Rapallo, Rome, Florence. Intollerance, impatience, differences; but never vanity. And all the while I was getting further and further from my theme. Pound's condition: places

1. « Confucius after twenty-four centuries stirs Pound into speech; Pound after twenty-four centuries lends Confucius his voice ». (Hugh Kenner, « Ezra Pound: Translations », a New Directions Paperbook, 1963).

2. Pound read the Ode « Na » from the Confucian Anthology, (which he had translated during his confinement in St. Elizabeth's, Washington D.C.) for a meeting of Poets held in the Caio Melisso Theatre, Spoleto, during the « Festival of Two Worlds ». (« The Confucian Odes ». Ezra Pound, Harvard University Press, 1954).

3. Carlo Scarfoglio: a neapolitan journalist and essayist; during the Fascist Regime he was suspended from journalistic activities. His translations of several of Pound's versions of the « Odes » appeared in « Nuova Antologia », ed. Antonio Baldini, 1958; his complete translation of the Confucian Anthology was published by Vanni Scheiwiller and Piero Draghi, ed. Pesce d'Oro, Milan, 1964, in a bilingual edition.

4. « A Lume Spento », Pound's first book, printed in Venice, 1908. The line referred to is from the poem « Vana ».

5. « Pisan Cantos »: Cantos 74-84, a section of Ezra Pound's « magnum opus » written during his imprisonment in the U.S.A. Disciplinary Camp at Coltano (Pisa) in 1945; published by « New Directions », New York and « Faber and Faber », London, awarded the « Bollingen Prize » by the Library of Congress, Washington D.C. in 1949.

6. « Men of Genius »: Arnold Bennett had refused to be represented in a book of portraits by the american photographer, A. L. Coburn, to be entitled « Men of Genius ». Coburn told the novelist that he would use another title if he would find him a better. « Men of Mark » was Bennett's alternative. (« Men of Mark », 32 portraits by A. L. Coburn, ed. Duckworth and Co, 1913).

7. Constantin Brancusi (1876-1957).

8. « Miglior fabbro » (Dante, Purgatorio XXVI, line 117) quoted by T. S. Eliot in his dedication of « The Waste Land » to Pound.

mentioned in the Pisan Cantos with Pound omitted! To this not inconsiderable difficulty which I might call « physical » was added a moral one. How should a reporter consider Ezra Pound. What should he look for?

The myth distorts the reality.

Pound, the man who has refused the myth as far as he could, by some occult contrary force becomes, ever increasingly, the great myth. Or, one might say the poet has constructed his myth against his will, in spite of his own wish, and as if he despised it. Add to his work of genius: generosity, humility, shyness - the human attributes. These photographic compositions will not give an exact evaluation of the Poet's personality. I agree with Pound's statement about exactitude in photography, made in relation to Brancusi's sculpture. (Little Review, 1921) [7].

Collaborations between writers and photographers usually create difficulties. My difficulties in this case were resolved by Pound's respect for the liberty of others. He vetoed anything in the book which might be considered as vanity; the second part of it he passed only out of consideration for my liberty. I am grateful to him. While compiling it I added, as it cropped up, evidence of Pound's more recent expressions of opinion.

To the man for men, to the poet for poets, to the « miglior fabbro » [8] of Imagism I dedicate these images:
    « Portraits of the Artist as an Old Man ».

And to all who have stood by me in this work, my thanks.

Vittorugo Contino

"well, my window
looked out on the squero where Ogni Santi
meets San Trovaso
things have ends and beginnings"
Canto LXXVI

> well, my window
>   looked out on the Squero where Ogni Santi
> meets San Trovaso
>   things have ends and beginnings
>   Canto LXXVI

The window of the room occupied by Pound in 1908, looks out
over *San Trovaso* canal on to one of the oldest boat yards in Venice,
the « *Squero* »; gondolas are still made and beached here for repairs.
The house door is in a side alley, Calle dei Frati, 942. « *A Lume
Spento* » was launched from here, at the author's own expense;
one hundred copies, printed by A. Antonini « in the city of Aldus »,
(Aldo Manuzio 1449-1515), as stated on the title page. *Ogni Santi*
canal is at right angles to that of San Trovaso.

"by the soap-smooth stone posts where San Vio
meets with the canal grande
between Salviati and the house that
shd/ I chuck the was of Don Carlos -
le bozze 'A Lume lot into the tide water ?
Spento'"

by the soap-smooth stone posts where San Vio
meets with il Canal Grande
between Salviati and the house that was of Don Carlos
shd/I chuck the lot into the tide-water?
        le bozze « A Lume Spento »

                        Canto LXXVI

« *The house that was of Don Carlos* »: - Palazzo *Loredan* on the
Grand Canal at Canal San Vio, then occupied by *Don Carlos*
(the « Carlist Pretender »). It is now the Venetian residence
of Count *Vittorio Cini*.

"with the new bridge of the Era where was the old eyesore

Canto LXXVI

with the new bridge of the Era where was the old eyesore

Canto LXXVI

After the First World War, a wooden bridge, _Ponte dell'Accademia,_
replaced the iron bridge of 1854.

"and in the font to the right as you enter
are all the gold domes of San Marco"

Canto XXXLXX VI

"and Tullio Lombardo carved the sirenes
as the old custode says: so that since
then no one has been able to carve them
for the jewel box, Santa maria dei Miracoli"
                                        LXXVI

and Tullio Romano carved the sirenes
         as the old custode says: so that since
then no one has been able to carve them
     for the jewel box, Santa Maria dei Miracoli,

                                        Canto LXXVI

« *Romano* » is a lapsus for « Lombardo ».
It should be remembered that while writing the Pisan Cantos in
the prison camp, Pound had no books other than a copy of the
Confucian Analects which he had in his pocket on arrival and had
been allowed to retain. In a previous Canto (XLI), Pound had
given the name correctly.

and in the font to the right as you enter
are all the gold domes of San Marco
                                   Canto LXXVI

« *and in the font to the right as you enter* » - a large porphyry
basin on a renaissance column, has been dry for many years and
its surrounding zinc gutter, now used for Holy Water, is too
narrow to reflect all the domes. It was refilled to allow
Contino to make this picture of the domes reflected in
the water as Pound had first seen them.

"Dei greci, San Giorgio, on place of skulls
, in the Carpaccio"
Canto LXXVI

Dei Greci, San Giorgio, the place of skulls
in the Carpaccio

Canto LXXVI

The Church of San Giorgio *dei Greci* is in close vicinage to
San Giorgio Schiavoni, a church of the Dalmatian Brotherood
were *Carpaccio* portrays the deeds of three Dalmatian saints:
St. George, St. Tryphonius and St. Jerome.
« the place of skulls » is in the lower left hand corner of the
painting, which depicts St. George and the dragon, with its victims.

Vôi che passate per questa via!
'Does D'Annunzio live here?'
    said the american lady, K.H.
'I do not know "said the ancient veneziana
'this lamp is for the virgin "
                                Canto LXXVI

Does D'Annunzio live here?
said the american lady, K. H.
    « I do not know » said the aged Veneziana,
        « this lamp is for the virgin. »

Canto LXXVI

« the american lady » was the pianist *Kathrine Ruth Heyman*.
Pound arranged a concert for her in the Benedetto Marcello
Concert Hall, in 1908, having borrowed it from Wolf Ferrari, then
Director of the Venetian Conservatory of Music.

" will I ever see the giudecca again ?

LXXVI

Will I ever see the Giudecca again?

Canto LXXXIII

the hidden nest, Tami's dream, the great Ovid
      bound in thick boards, the bas relief of Ixotta

Canto LXXVI

«The hidden nest, Tami's dream» - «Tami's dream»: a large abstract
painting by the japanese artist, *Tami Koume,* a Paris friend of Pound's
during the early twenties. He is reported to have disappeared in the
japanese earthquake of 1923. When Pound gave up his Paris studio,
in rue Nôtre Dame des Champs, he sent the painting, with another
smaller one by Koume, to a friend in Auteuil. In 1931 they were
brought to Venice. The *«hidden nest»* was sequestrated as alien enemy
property during the last World War and the paintings «disappeared»
as did the *« great Ovid »* (Ovid's « Fasti » printed by a successor
of Bodoni) which Pound had bought from the venetian antiquarian
bookseller, Sig. Cassini, and had had bound in wooden covers.
The *« bas relief of Ixotta »,* a small marble plaque of Ixotta degli
Atti (Canto IX), he had had cemented to the wall where it still is.
Beside the Ixotta plaque, the photograph shows reproductions of a
drawing by Kokoschka of Pound and of his portrait by Wyndham
Lewis (Tate Gallery, London).

" and the Canal Grande has lasted
    at least until our time "
                Canto LXXVI

and the Canal Grande has lasted at least until our time

Canto LXXVI

" Can Grande's grin like Tommy Cochran's "

Can Grande's grin like Tommy Cochran's

Canto LXXVIII

The reference is to the equestrian statue of *Can Grande della Scala*
surmounting his tomb outside the church of Santa Maria Antica
in Verona.
« *Tommy Cochran* »: « just a nice kid I knew in Wyncote »
(circa 1900), E. P. in conversation.

So he said, looking at the signed columns in San Zeno

So he said, looking at the signed columns in San Zeno
« how the hell can we get any architecture
                    when we order our columns by the gross? »
red marble with a stone loop cast round it, four shafts

                    Canto LXXVIII

The speaker is *Ed. Williams,* architect brother of William Carlos
Williams; he and Pound were in Verona together in 1911.

a cuius invigilantia totius
bonum erectum est; A...
...um et Provincia Cives et
...auis ab hinc annis gra...
...m, eenuuum fratribus et
...n potie annuis prestation...
...bona tam grandi fenore

...citatis, eiusq[ue] Itomenis com=

advertens aniuersos fere

...colas ob pecunia scarcita-

pressos are alieno et tam=

...reris, licet legitimis consump-

...tas satisfacere req[ue] famili-

...ficatas; immo in dies magis

/2

*"and credit, Siena;
with for the trust and the mistrust;
'the earth belongs to the living'.*
                                        Canto LXXVII

... and Credit, *Siena;*
both for the trust and the mistrust;
« the earth belongs to the living ».

Canto LXXVII

The reference is to the *Monte dei Paschi* of Siena, an old and
famous Bank. In the Fifth Decade of Cantos (subtitle: Siena and
The Leopoldine Reforms) Pound gives the history of the
transformation of the *Monte di Pietà,* founded 1472, into an
Institution of Credit based on the « *Paschi* », the grazing lands in the
Maremma, in 1624. *The Monte dei Paschi* is given as an example
of sound banking in contrast to Banks which « create money out
of nothing ».

« *Thus the BANK of the Grasslands was raised into Seignory, 1622* ».

The last of the strictly Sienese Cantos ends with the lines:

*The foundation, Siena, has been to keep bridle on usury
        Nicolò Piccolomini, Provveditore*

« *With Usura* » (Canto XLV) follows immediately and Canto LII
starts with a recapitulation:

> « *And I have told you of how things were under Duke*
> > *Leopold in Siena*
> *And of the true base of credit, that is*
> > *the abundance of nature*
> *with the whole folk behind it* ».

" with Maria's face there in the fresco "
Canto LXXXIII

With Maria's face there in the fresco

Canto LXXXIII

The « *face* » is in a painting, probably late seventeenth century,
which reminded Pound of his daughter's face. He was staying in
Palazzo Capoquadri Salimbene and noticed it in a panel over
one of the doors of the large hall. The same « child's face » is alluded
to in Canto LXXIV as is « Montino's », the young son of Prince
Ranieri di San Faustino, whose resemblance to one of his family,
in a painting, « the family group 1820 », brought to Pound's
mind Hardy's poem « The family face ». He comments; « not wholly
Hardy's material ».

*and I trust they have not destroyed the
old theatre*

by restaurations, and by late renaissance ghiribizzi
dov'è Barilli?

Canto LXXX

The « *old theatre* » (Teatro dei Rinnovati) forms part of the Palazzo
Pubblico in the Piazza del Campo, Siena. First used in 1560 it
was reconstructed by Bibbiena in 1783. During the first « Sienese
Music Week », 1939, Alfredo Casella brought a group of friends and
journalists to see the building, long in disuse, to get backing for its
restoration; *Barilli* (Bruno Barilli, 1880-1952, critic and composer)
and Pound met and became friends on this occasion. « Dove è
Barilli? » (« where is Barilli? ») recalls the « Torquato where art
thou? » of Canto LXXIV. (Manlio Torquato Dazzi, poet and
man of letters, another friend).

as the grass on the roof of St What's his name
near « Cane e Gatto ».

Canto LXXXIII

The Saint is *San Giorgio,* in Pantaneto, and *« Cane e Gatto »,*
« Dog and Cat » a nearbye meeting of narrow streets. The traditional
Procession which carries the wax offerings to the Madonna takes
place the day before the August Palio and it forms in front of the
Church, (see Canto LXIII). Palazzo Capoquadri Salimbene has
windows which give on the proceedings; the first floor windows
from which Pound watched them are about level with the church roof.

"and the tossing of the flags of the Contrade"

Canto LXXX

and the tossing of the flags of the contrade

Canto LXXX

" snow on the marble
snow -white
against the stone-white "

              snow on the marble
snow-white
         against stone-white
                                    Canto LXXXIV

"The Pisan clouds are undoubtedly various
and splendid as any I have seen
since at Scudder's Falls
on the Schuylkill"

The Pisan clouds are undoubtedly various
        and splendid as any I have seen since
at Scudder's Falls on the Schuylkill

Canto LXXVII

« *Scudder's Falls:* » a stretch of a tributary of the Delaware, last
seen by Pound in his early twenties when he was tutoring
a youth of the Scudder family.
In Canto LXXIV *clouds* are recalled several times; « on wet days
clouds banked on Taishan »; « pale as the dawn cloud »;
« cloud over mountain mountain over cloud »; out of a cloud's
mountain; « and the clouds near to Pisa »; « no cloud, but the
crystal body »; « the clouds over the Pisan meadows »; and in
Canto LXXVI: « the cloud *dove sta memora* ».

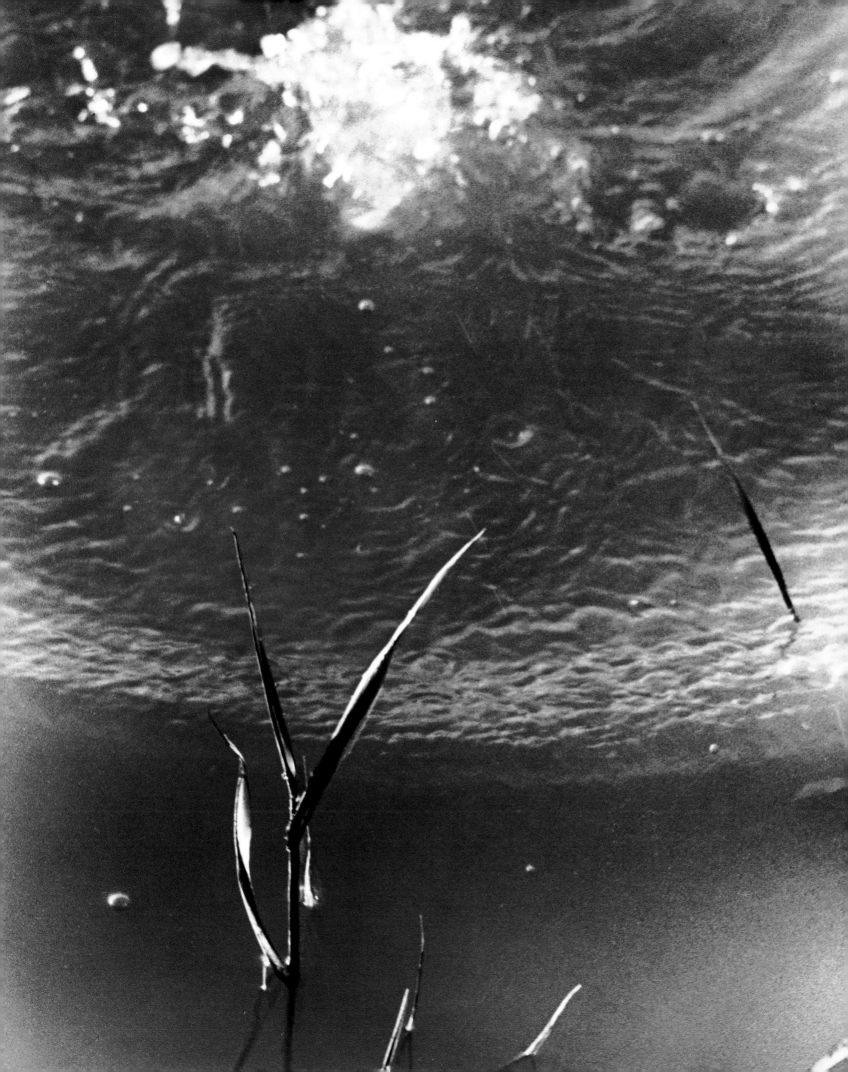

"when the mind swings by a grass-blade"

When the mind swings by a grass-blade

Canto LXXXIII

Recurring all through the Cantos, *grass* is mentioned most often
in the « Pisans »: (Canto LXXIV) « Grass, nowhere out of place »;
« the dwarf morning-glory twines round the grass-blade »;
« grass worn from its root hold »; « but as grass under Zephirus
as the green˙blade under Apeliota »; « and this grass, or whatever,
here under the tent flaps is, indubitably, bambooiform »; and in
Canto LXXVI; « lay in soft grass by the cliff's edge ». Carpaccio
borders his « place of skulls » with coarse grass separating it from
the idyllic landscape in the upper half of the picture.

"Nor can who has passed a month
in the death cells
believe in capital punishment

'No man who has passed a month
in the death cells
believes in cages for beasts

Nor can who has passed a month in the death cells
    believe in capital punishment
No man who has passed a month in the death cells
    believes in cages for beasts

            Canto LXXXIII

The iron cages (American Disciplinary Training Centre) in one of which Pound, « incomunicado », without books or letters, planned his Pisan Cantos. By day he could watch the Pisan clouds, at night, lying on the cement floor, he had the moon for « pin-up ».

"O moon my pin-up"

O moon my pin-up,

Canto LXXXIV

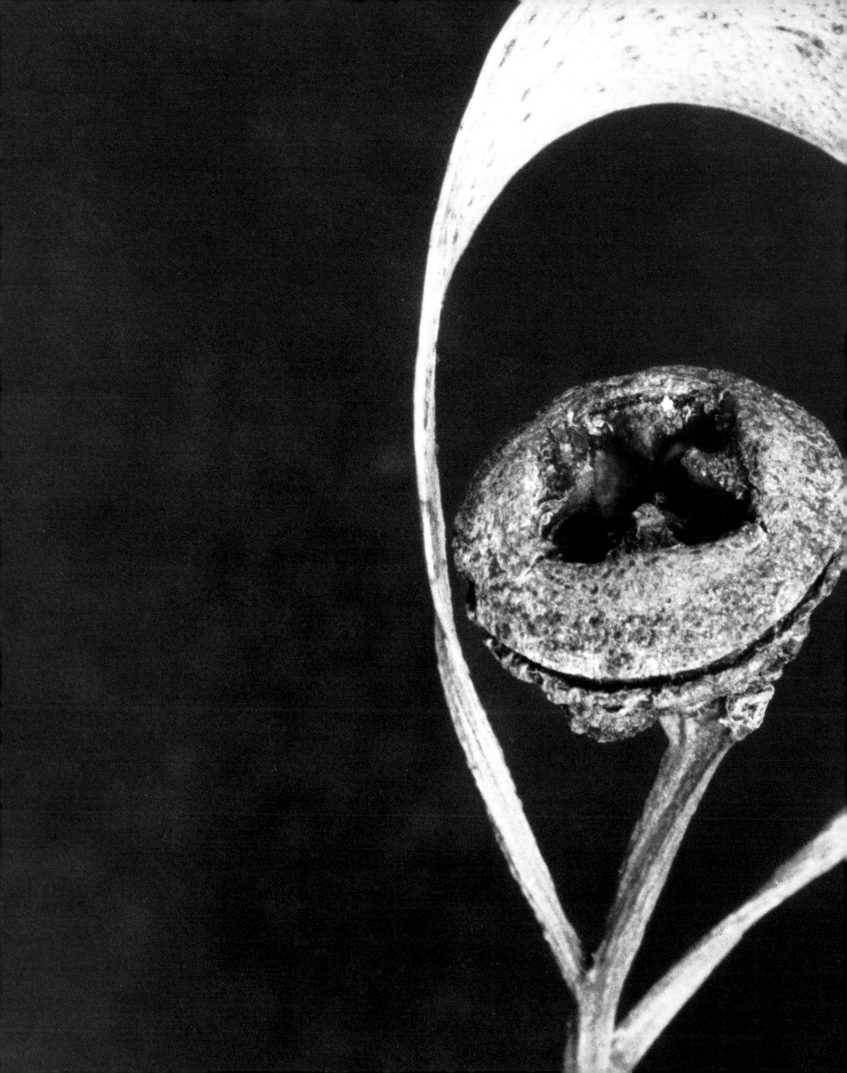

island eucalyptus   that is for memory...

and eucalyptus that is for memory
under the olives, by cypress, mare Tirreno,

Canto LXXIV

Eucalyptus trees grow by the « old mule path » leading up from
Rapallo to Sant'Ambrogio and San Pantaleo and down into Zoagli.
Half way up, one large tree, so close to a tall cypress as seemingly
to grow from the same root, is a land-mark known as « L'eucalipto ».
The beauty of the spot is now marred by the ever encroaching
cement. On his climb up, Pound would pocket an odd eucalyptus
« pip » and had one in his pocket when he was locked in the cage
at the Pisan Camp. He recalls the « eucalyptus » theme repeatedly:
« one eucalyptus pip from the salita that goes up from Rapallo »
(Canto LXXX); this follows a reference to Thomas Hardy's letter
Pound had in his pocket on leaving England, and the $80 in his
pocket on leaving for Europe as a young man. « The cat-faced
eucalyptus nib is where you cannot get at it », a line addressed to
a prowling cat in the Camp (LXXX); « the eucalyptus bobble is
missing » (Canto LXXX); « the odour of eucalyptus »
(Canto LXXX); and as variants on « pip »: « nib », « bobble »,
« cat-faced », « croce di Malta » (maltese cross), « figura del sol »
(sun-faced).

"no vestige save in the air
in stone is no imprint
and the grey walls of no era
under the olives."

no vestige save in the air
in stone is no imprint and the grey walls of no era
under the olives

Canto LXXIV

the olives grey over grey holding-walls
and their leaves turn under Scirocco

the olives grey over grey holding walls
and their leaves turn under Scirocco

Canto LXXVI

"under the grey cliff in periplum"

under the grey cliff in periplum

Canto LXXIV

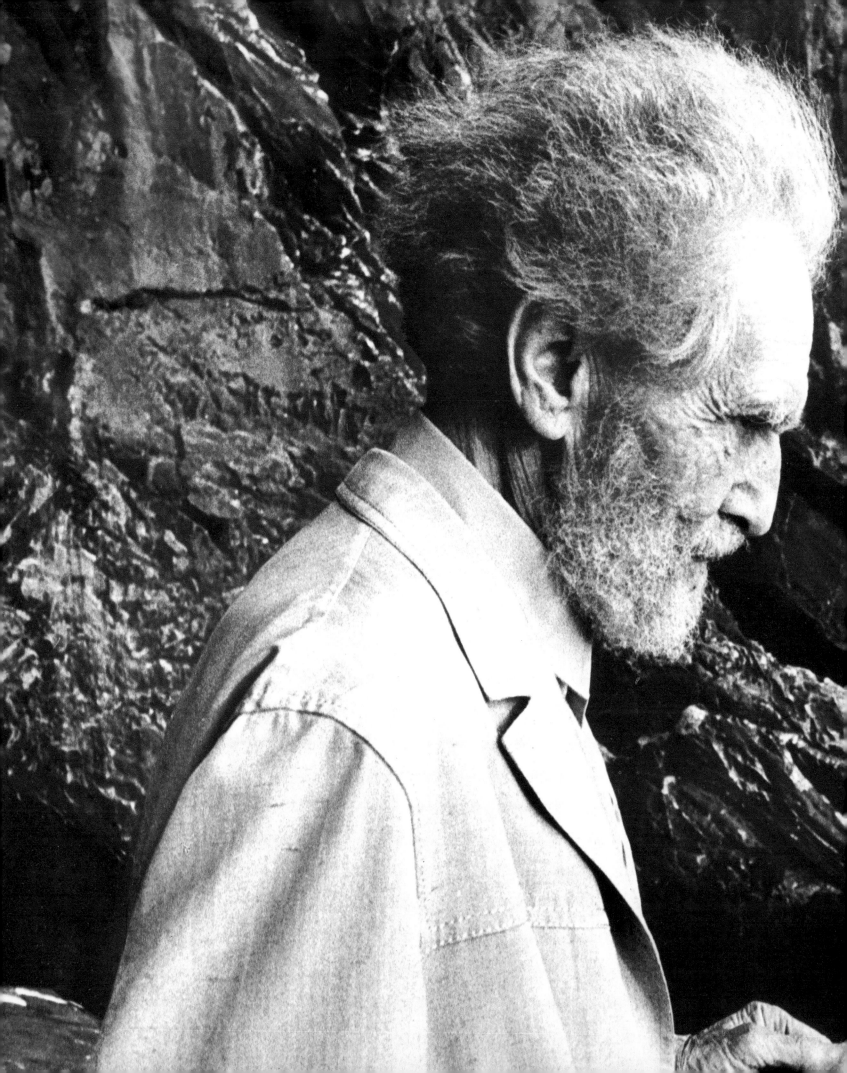

*I don't know how humanity stands it
with a painted paradise at the end of it
without a painted paradice at the
end of it "*

I don't know how humanity stands it
with a painted paradise at the end of it
without a painted paradise at the end of it

Canto LXXIV

In the Church of S. Ambrogio above Rapallo.

The « salita » Sant'Ambrogio; the poet's house in the back ground.

*The squares are too even... Theatre of war...
theatre' is good. there are those who did not
want it
to come To an end"*

The chess board too lucid
the squares are too even... theatre of war...
« theatre » is good. There are those who did not want
it to come to an end

Canto LXXVIII

See; « *Game of Chess* » Dogmatic Statement Concerning the
Game of Chess: Theme for a series of pictures, Lustra (1912).

Ara Pacis
Roma

While compiling this book I tried to include,
as it cropped up, evidence of Pound's
more recent expressions of opinion.
The following photographs show texts which,
translated, were used for an Italian
documentary film. To facilitate his speaking
in a language not his own Pound stipulated
that he read his answers to the
Italian writers interviewing him.

(*V. C.*)

Ezra Pound and Pier Paolo Pasolini had met briefly at a Literary Congress in Sicily but had never conversed. Their second meeting was in Pound's Venice studio where Alfredo Di Lauro was filming a documentary for the Rome Television. Pasolini's opening gambit was to read lines from Pound's early poem, « A Pact »; « I make a pact with you Walt Whitman, I have detested you long enough... I come to you as a grown child/ who has had a pig-headed father/I am old enough now to make friends ». And he added: « I could read this "I make a pact with you Ezra Pound". Have you any comment? » Pound's answer;

«All right — friends! Pax tibi - Pax mundi».

Pasolini was sketching as he talked; he quoted from Canto LXXVI: « Woe to them that conquer with armies and whose only right is their power » saying: « These are pacificist verses. Would you like to participate in one of the demonstrations which are taking place in America to help the world remain at peace? » And Pound answered:

« In reply to your question; I think the intentions are good, but I do not think these demonstration are the right answer. I see things from another angle. As I wrote in a draft for a recent Canto; « When one's friends hate one another/how can there be peace in the world ».

And to a question about a passage in Canto LXXVIII: « In "the Spring and Autumn" there are no righteous wars », the answer was: « Spring and Autumn' is a book attributed to Confucius, who certainly did not consider war a universal panacea ».

On Pasolini's asking was he thinking of himself when he wrote; « The young Dumas weeps because the young Dumas has tears », he replied: « No, by "the young Dumas" I was not thinking of myself; in the Pisan Cantos I wrote; « Tard, très tard, je t'ai connue, la tristesse / I have been hard as youth sixty years ».

The answers to Vanni Ronsisvalle follow. He had asked Pound's advice to the young:

« Curiosity — advice to the young — curiosity ».

To Ronsisvalle's supposition that he had traveled a great deal: « I have not done much travelling, in fact I have stayed put for years at a time. I don't see that restlessness is necessary for artists or for anyone ».

To the suggestion that literature may spring from hate, Pound answered;

« part of literature seems to spring from hate but its vitality is not in the hatred ».

Ronsisvalle tried to turn the conversation to Joyce in Paris, but Pound was under a more recent impression:

« When I was in Zurich in the winter of '67 I saw Joyce's bare grave — other graves had little Christmas trees and wreathes with candles as is the custom there. Joyce's name with Nora's nearly illegible on a stone hidden in the grass'

To a question about Paris in the 1920's:

You ask about my Paris friends in the 1920's: Brancusi, Joyce, Hemingway. Stein, whom you mention, I knew very slightly.

Brancusi seemed to me a saint, he is first in my list of values in « Guide to Kulcher ». I want to see his Table of Silence, a venetian friend has offered to take me to Roumania to see it.

Hemingway did not disappoint me.

Cocteau called me the rower on the river of the dead: « le rameur sur la fleuve des morts »; it is sad to look back.

At the end of the conversation Pound read an Ode from his version of the Confucian Anthology commencing: « Folk worn out, workin so late ».

curiosity – advice to a young –
curiosity

curiosity - advice to the young - curiosity

curiosity - advice to the young - *curiosity*

part of literature seems to spring from hate but its vitality is not in the hatred.

" Folk worn out, workin' so late,
Kind rule at center
Pitch out the hands on a state.
slitheers—
and scare off worse,
thieves and thugs see a
light and a curse;
(Anima Floid)
Put Easy on for men;
do with what's near,
And the thing can sit easy quiet
the rest of the year "
(Decade of Sheng min)
Confucian Odes

Part of literature seems to spring from hate but its vitality is not in the hatred.

« Folk worn out, workin' so late,
kind rulè at center
                    hauls on a state,
pitch out the slimers,
                    and scare off worse,
thieves and thugs see a light and curse;
easy on far men,
                    do with what's near,
and the king can sit quiet
                    the rest of the year ».

(Decade of Sheng Min) *Confucian Odes*

Spring and Autumn is a book
attributed to Confucius, who
certainly did not consider war
a universal panacea.

No, by the « young Dumas » I was not
thinking of myself; in the Pisan
Cantos I wrote:
« tard, très tard, je t'ai connue,
la tristesse ».

"Spring and Autumn" is a title attributed to Confucius, who certainly did not consider war a universal panacea.

—

No, "jy'd young Damas" I was not thinking of myself; in a Pisan Cantos I wrote:

tard, très tard, je t'ai connue la tristesse."

you ask about my Paris friends
in the 1920's — Brancusi, Joyce,
Hemingway. Stein whom
whom you mention, I knew very
slightly.

Brancusi seemed to me a saint.
he is first in my list of values
in my .... "guide to Balchair
I want to see his Table of
Silence. a Venetian friend has
offered to take me to Roumania
to see it.

Hemingway did not disappoint me.
Cocteau called me a "rower on the
river of do the dead", "le
rameur sur la fleuve des droits
morts". it is sad sad to look
back.

You ask about my Paris friends
in the 1920's: Brancusi, Joyce,
Hemingway. Stein, whom you mention,
I knew very slightly.

Brancusi seemed to me a saint,
he is first in my list of values
in « Guide to Kulcher ».
I want to see his Table of
Silence, a venetian friend has
offered to take me to Roumania
to see it.

Hemingway did not disappoint me.

Cocteau called me the rower on the
river of the dead: « le rameur sur la fleuve des
morts »; it is sad to look
back.

All right — friends!
Pax tibi - Pax mundi.

In reply to your question;
I think the intentions are good, but
I do not think these demonstrations
are the right aswer. I see things
from another angle. As I wrote in a draft for a recent Canto;
   « when one's friends hate one another
   how can there be peace in the world ».

I have not done much travelling,
in fact I have stayed put for years
at a time. I don't see that restlessness
is necessary for artists or for anyone.

all right — friends!
pax tibi pax mundi

in reply to your question:
I think the intentions are good, but
I do not think these demonstrations
are the right answer. I see things
from another angle. As I wrote in
a draft for a recent canto:
"when one's friends hate one another
"how can there be peace in the world."

I have not done much traveling,
in fact I have stayed put for years
at a time. I don't see that restlessness
is necessary for artists or for any one.

when I was in Zürich in the winter
of 67 I saw Joyce's bare grave —
other graves had little christmas tree
trees and wreaths with candles
as is the custom there. Joyce's name
with Nora's nearly illegible
in a stone hidden in the grass.

When I was in Zurich in the winter
of '67 I saw Joyce's bare grave -
other graves had little Christmas
trees and wreathes with candles
as is the custom there. Joyce's name
with Nora's nearly illegible
on a stone hidden in the grass.

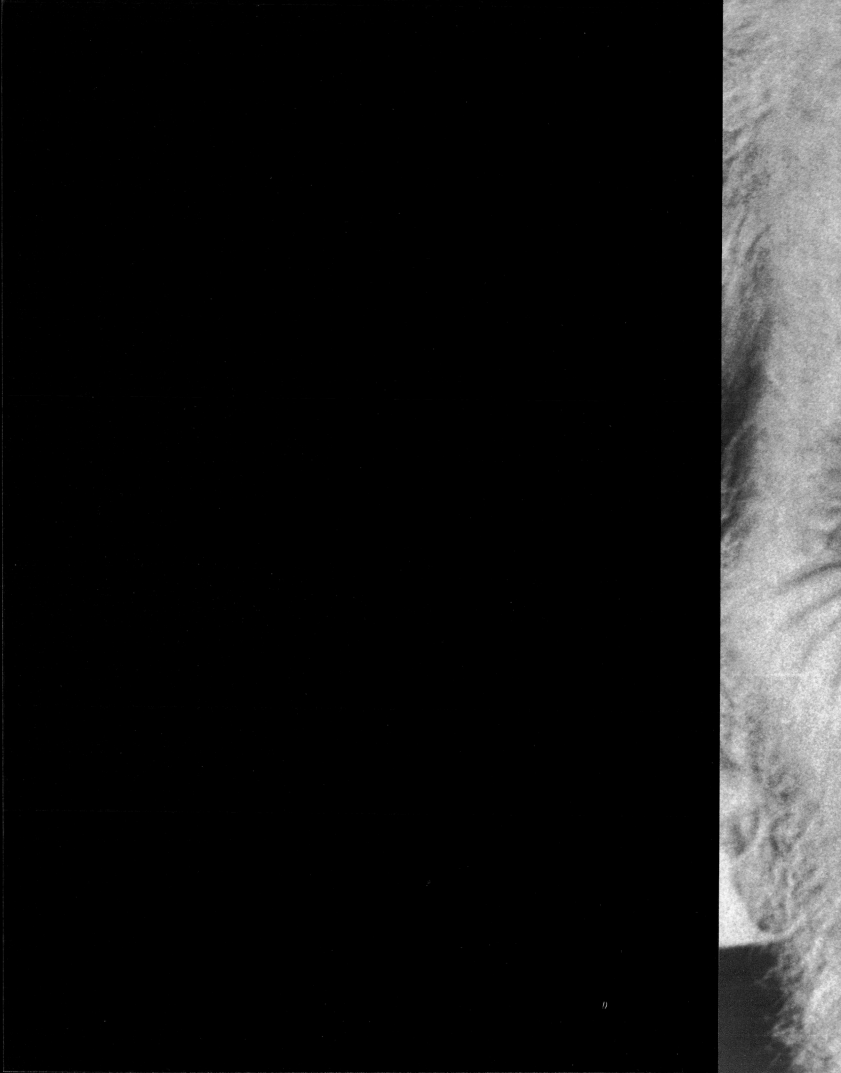

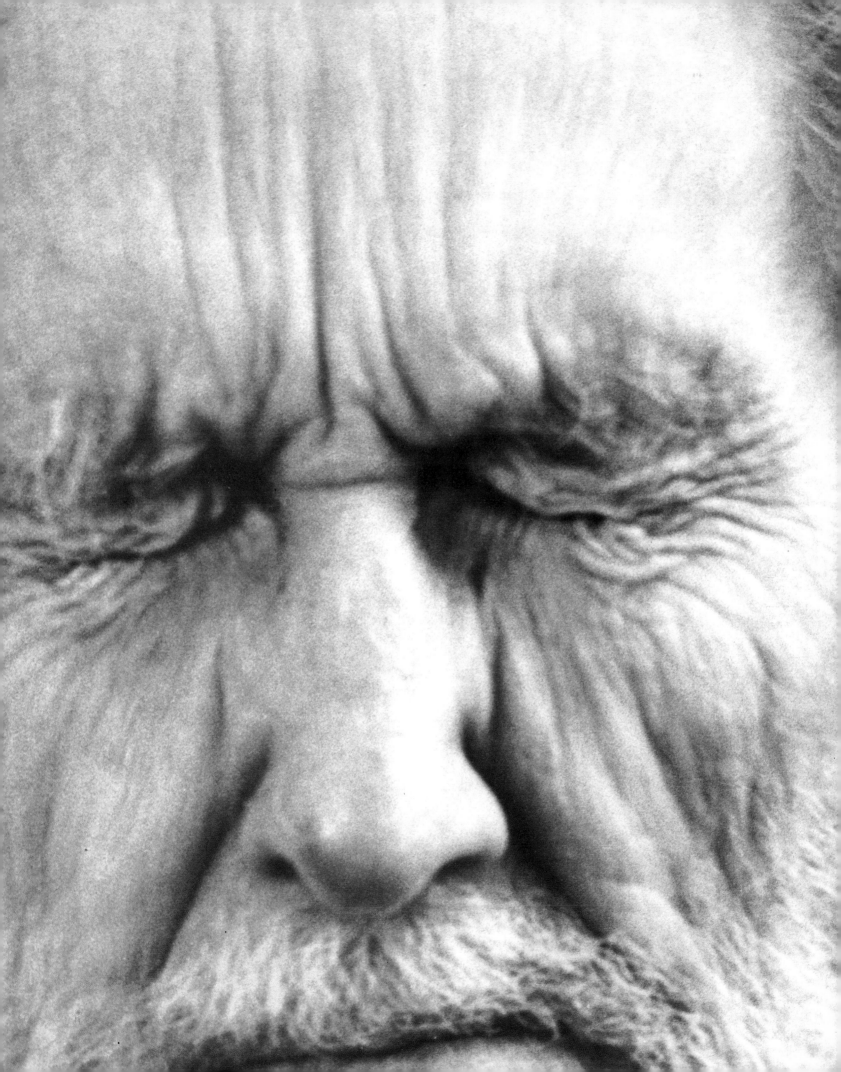

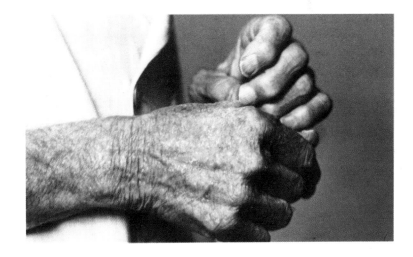

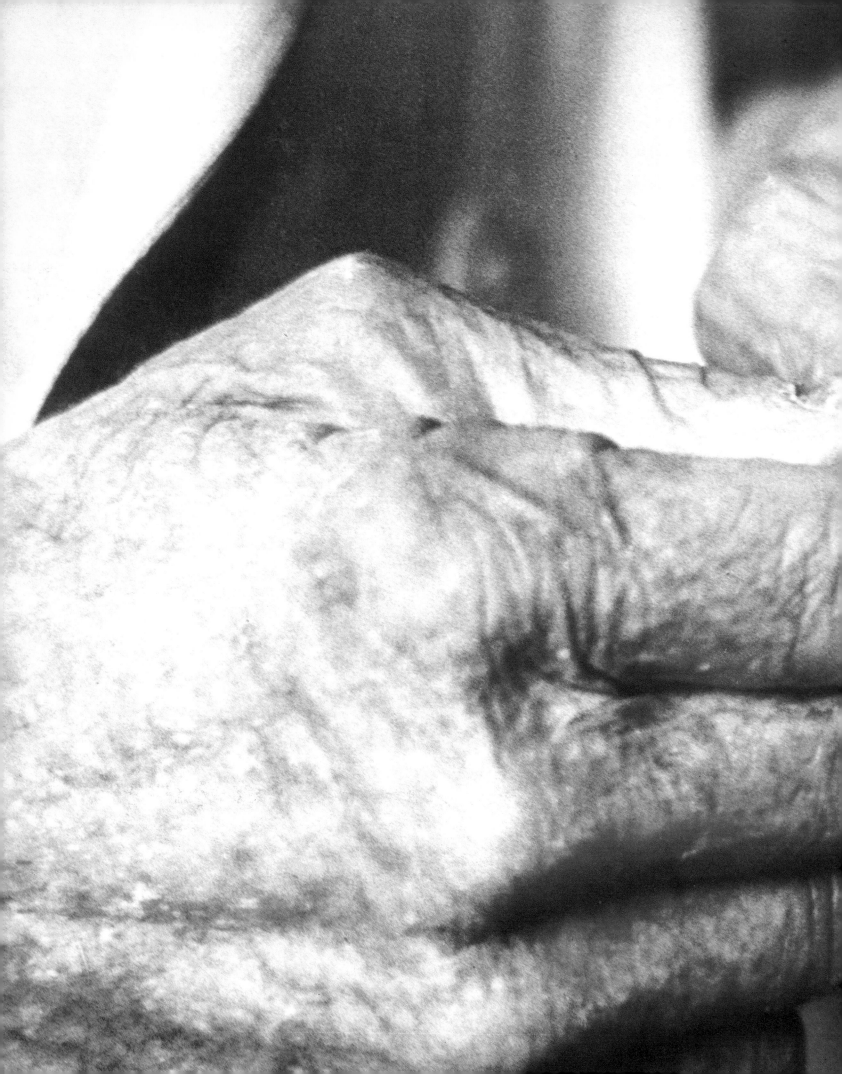

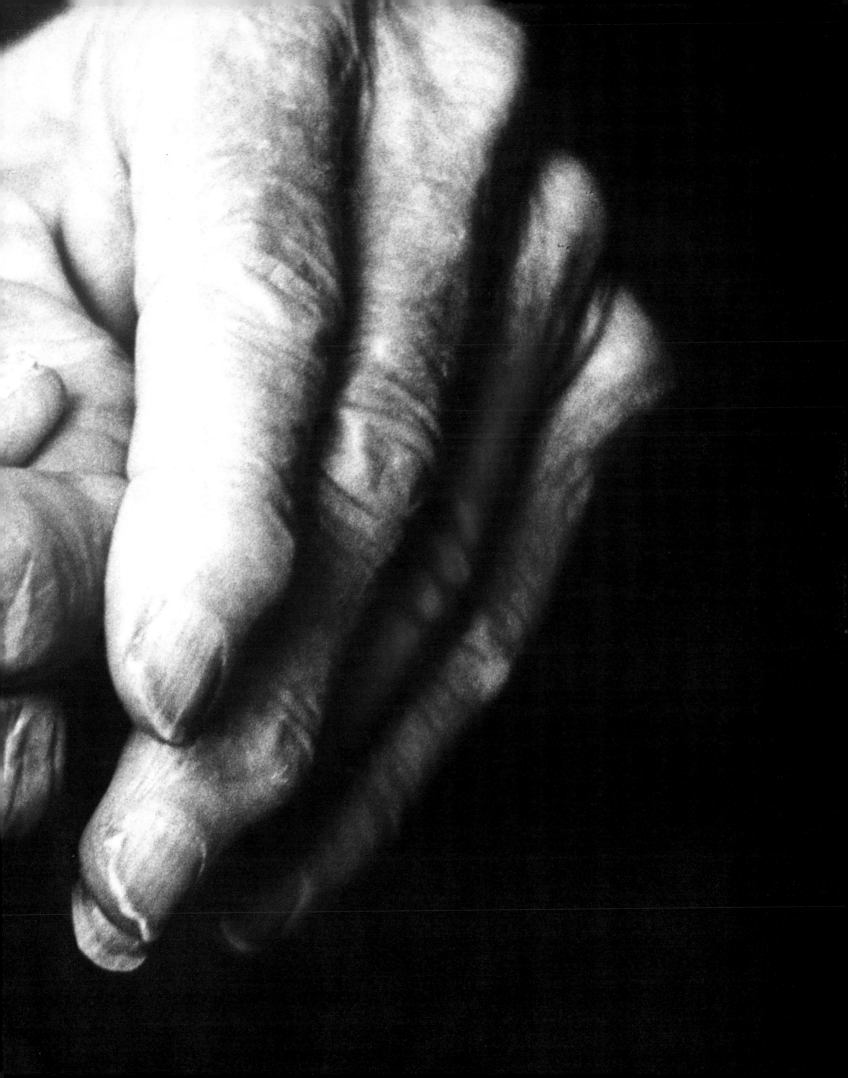

A birthday in Venice.

"Make strong the old dreams
lest this our world lose heart"

(1908)   *A Lume Spento*

Ezra Pound

Make strong the old dreams
least this our world lose heart
« A Lume Spento »

Vittorugo Contino who was born in Palermo in 1925 now lives in Rome. After completing studies in Industrial Engineering and Architecture he turned to Photography, taking a degree in Optics in 1952 at the Experimental Centre for Cinematography of Rome. His technique is based on these studies, and his pictures are the result of repeated experiment.

His interests include music and science and his particular research is in the field of contemporary history and has covered: war in the middle east, 1956; Algiers 1959; Viet Nam 1965; Youth-cultures in the Orient and in the Occident, 1965, and Spanish Festivals, 1965-66 as well as Italian Folk-lore, 1966-67. Since 1963, Contino is a member of the A.S.M.P.

« Ezra Pound in Italy » (from the Pisan Cantos) grew out of a friendly relationship of some years during which Contino registered images inspired by the Cantos during visits with Pound to places recorded in them.

PISAN CANTOS
some translations

The Pisan Cantos - first published by James Laughlin,
"New Directions", New York, 1948,
and in London by Faber & Faber 1949.

Canti Pisani - Italian translation by Alfredo Rizzardi,
ed. Ugo Guanda, Parma, 1953.

Die Pisaner Gesänge - German translation by Eva Hesse,
ed. "Im Verlag der Arche", Zurich, 1956.

Los Cantares de Pisa - Spanish translation by José Vazquez Amaral,
"Imprenta Universitaria", Mexico.

Sånger från Pisa - Sweedish Translation by Göran Sonnevi
& Jan Olov Ullén,
"Bo Cavefors Bokförlag", Malmö-Lund.

Cantos Pisans - French translation by Denis Roche,
ed. "L'Herne, D. de Roux", Paris.

Printed in Italy
by Grafiche Le.Ma. - Maniago - Pn - 1978